Editor's Note

The editor, already familiar with the facts regarding Medjugorje, prepared herself, at the invitation of some friends, to offer to the reader a documentary of these happenings by means of a portfolio of images. What remained was to bring together in a single collection a series of magical snapshots of the protagonists of those extraordinary and unrepeatable moments during one of their encounters with the Madonna, and of the places in which these events were transpiring.

While awaiting the judgment of the competent ecclesiastical authorities, the editor, out of a sense of duty to inform, wants to participate in the diffusion of news regarding these experiences already known to some extent throughout the world, and she has chosen to do so by means of this collection of several excerpts from the many messages which, in that place, were given for all the people of our time.

The subject treated here and the impressions left by the photographs themselves cannot leave indifferent the reader who, certainly free to express himself or herself in favor of or against the experience of an entire populace, might feel encouraged to go to Medjugorje to strengthen or disprove the testimony of many who, as pilgrims to that place, have returned with their own faith re-found or reinforced.

Emanuele

Medjugorje
A Portfolio of Images

ALBA HOUSE — 2187 Victory Boulevard
Staten Island, New York 10314

The original edition of this book was published in 1985
by Bertoncello Artigrafiche, Cittadella (Padova), Italy
under the Title: *Un evento per immagini* — **Medjugorje**.

The English language version follows the French edition:
Medjugorje — *Images d'un événement*.
Translated by Edmund C. Lane, S.S.P.

Printed in January, 1987, from type set in the U.S.A.
ISBN: 0-8189-0516-6

© Bertoncello Artigrafiche, Cittadella (Padova), Italy

A special thanks is extended to the following who
have collaborated in the elaboration of this collec-
tion of photographs and messages:
G. Amorth, A. Baron, F. Bellini, A. Bonifacio,
A. Frassinelli, A. Gava, U. Manenti, A. Muti,
M. Paccagnan, F. Paravicini, R. Parovel,
T. Pasquazzo, M. Rastrelli, M. Valenta, and
F. Vatta.

*This collection is dedicated
to all generous young people
to whom the Virgin Mary
has confidently entrusted
the future of humanity.*

Printed in Italy

Bertoncello Artigrafiche, Cittadella (Padova)

Table of Contents

Introduction

The facts are already known and all the world has been informed that since June 24, 1981 at Medjugorje, a little village in the Province of Bosnia-Herzegovina, Yugoslavia, the Madonna is said to have been appearing to six young teenagers. Well over a thousand of these apparitions, beginning initially on Podbrdo hill, then on Mt. Krizevać, followed successively by appearances in the sacristy of the parish church, in the homes of the seers, in several parts of the country and, finally, in whatever place the visionaries might have found themselves at the hour established for these encounters (6:00-6:15 p.m.).

Through these youngsters, the Blessed Virgin is bringing her message of conversion and peace to the world, saying that these will be her last apparitions on earth. And she has invited all men and women of good will to fast and pray, to frequent the sacrament of the Eucharist and that of Reconciliation, for too long neglected: *"Take my message seriously, for God is not joking with mankind."*

She is said to have promised that she would entrust to the six seers ten secrets and that she would leave a tangible and visible sign on the hill of the first apparitions for atheists, that they, too, might come to believe. She has likewise assured the children that humanity will be freed from the power of evil when the contents of all the secrets have been fulfilled. Then a new era of peace and a faith-filled return to God will be initiated on the earth. The people of the valley of Medjugorje, a people of ancient and lively faith, have taken the message of the Madonna to heart and put it into practice with a great sense of responsibility, witnessing their interior transformation by their changed lives. This people, which for 400 years defended their faith against all contamination, often at the cost of their own blood, love to call themselves, "Roman Catholics, faithful to the Pope and to the Apostolic Church."

The Blessed Virgin specifically chose to appear in the parish of Medjugorje in order that the Croatian people, renewed in the faith, might be a sign and an invitation to conversion for all peoples, and that the teenage prayer group, led by her through two children gifted with "interior locution," might become a stimulus for others to live an intense spiritual life, allowing themselves to be led towards the summits of prayer.

At Medjugorje the visionaries and the inhabitants of that little village are not just watching in wonder at what has been happening, but everyone close to those prophetic voices are equally vigilant regarding their practice of the faith and their adherence to the Gospel.

How long will these apparitions continue? No one can know God's plan. We do know that the Madonna is said to have repeated insistently: *"Thank God the Father that he has granted me the possibility of remaining in your midst for so long. Thank Him, too, that the first part of the plan of salvation has been realized. Now you must help me with your prayer and fasting so that the second might be brought to a successful conclusion."*

"Peace! Peace! Peace! . . . and only Peace!"

"My peace be with you!" says the Risen Lord. (Jn 20:19)

This is the dominant and insistent message of Mary to the seers, who were anxious to know her name. *"I AM THE QUEEN OF PEACE!"* she revealed.
It is the message to which the Blessed Virgin Mary called the greatest attention and which heaven itself confirmed on the night of June 25, 1981 when the extraordinary and luminous sign with the word MIR (=Peace) appeared written in large letters across the sky between Mount Krizevać and Podbrdo hill, highly visible to the pastor and to the inhabitants of all the valley.

"Peace, peace! But there is no peace!" (Jr 6:14)

The rocky summit of Podbrdo where the first of the apparitions took place. Pilgrims in prayer.

And her invitation for peace is not deprived of sense.

The Virgin repeats it every day with the patience of a Mother who, seeing the world full of *"such tensions,"* clearly admonishes it: *"If the world keeps on going in this way, it will soon find itself on the edge of ruin. It will find salvation only in peace, which it can have only if it will find God. God exists! Tell that to everyone. Those who listen to God will possess peace with themselves and with others, and they will have life. . . . In God divisions do not exist . . . and there are not many religions. It is you in the world who have created divisions. . . . Jesus is the sole Mediator. . . ."*

"Do what He tells you!"

(Jn 2:5)

The panorama which the summit of Podbrdo dominates; at the center can be seen the parish church.

The crowd outside participates at the celebration of the Mass which is taking place in the parish church at Medjugorje. In the background, at the left is Krizevać.

"In those days, Jesus went by himself alone to a mountain where he spent the night in prayer." (Lk 6:12)

Mary, the first and most faithful of the disciples of the Lord, at Medjugorje does no more than draw the attention of mankind to the Gospel of Jesus and to the Jesus of the Gospel: *"You have forgotten that with prayer and fasting you can even keep war at bay, you can suspend the laws of nature. So start to pray. You are weak in faith because you pray so little."* Like a wise teacher, she suggests that they start little by little, with a minimum of seven "Our Father"s, "Hail Mary"s, "Glory Be"s and a "Creed"; with a fast of bread and water on Fridays, because without *prayer and fasting* conversion is difficult, and without conversion one cannot live in communion with God and one's brothers and sisters.

The seers in ecstasy during an apparition. From left to right: Vicka, Jakov, Ivanka, Mirjana, Marija, Ivan.

The conversion proposed by the Blessed Virgin — with the purpose of realizing the command of Jesus, "Love your enemies. . . . pray for those who mistreat you" (Lk 6:27-28) — is the fruit of grace and of a superabundant effusion of the love of God in one's heart.

For that reason, it is necessary that we plead with incessant, confident prayer, that the Sacred Heart of Jesus might pour forth upon us this grace and love, and that through His mediation it might bear abundant fruit in us.

Mary reassures us in this regard: *"In your prayer, I ask you to turn to Jesus. I am your Mother, and I will intercede with Him on your behalf."* Who, in fact, knows better than she the fidelity of her Son to these, His own words: "If you, wicked as you are, know how to give good things to your children, how much more will your Father in heaven give the Holy Spirit (that is, the gift of Love) to those who ask Him for it" (Lk 11:23)?

The seers make the sign of the cross at the beginning of their ecstasy.

group of the faithful gathered together in the parish church of St. James.

"Pray together as a family"

"**I** would be very happy if families would begin to pray together for a half hour in the morning and in the evening."

"Don't look to hear extraordinary voices; take up the Gospels and read them. . . . There everything is clear. . . Pray! Don't ask why I keep imploring you to pray always."

"Intensify your personal prayers and this will redound to the benefit of others."

"I am your good Mother and Jesus is your best Friend. . . . Don't be afraid, but give Him your heart and tell Him about all your sufferings."

"Thus will you be revitalized through prayer, with your heart set free and at peace."

A family at prayer at 6:00 in the morning.

16

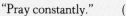

"**D**ear children, I invite you to renew the prayer life of your families; encourage the other children to pray and the toddlers to go to Mass. Prayer must be given first place. . . . Why don't you abandon yourselves to my care? I want you to lead lives of prayer . . . With the five 'Our Father's, 'Hail Mary's, 'Glory Be's, and the 'Creed', unite your prayer to that of the Holy Spirit. And if it is possible, it would be good for you to recite at least a third of the Rosary. . . There is no limit to prayer. . . . Pray, therefore. . . . Thus faith will be reborn in you and you will enjoy much happiness. . . . When I say to you: Pray! Pray! Pray! I don't only mean for you to get together when you pray, but I want to bring you to a continuous longing for God."

The two youngsters who enjoy "interior locutions." At the left is Marijana, and next to her is Jelena with her little sister.

Meetings with two Bishops

The miraculous event which has made the greatest stir is the instantaneous healing of Mrs. Diana Basile.

Born in 1940, married and the mother of three children, Diana has been afflicted since 1972 with multiple sclerosis aggravated by diverse problems: a serious difficulty in walking, the nearly complete immobility of her right arm, urinary incontinence, etc.

On May 23, 1984, she made a pilgrimage to Medjugorje. "I found myself on the sidewalk just outside the church. A lady from Bologna helped me up the steps. I had no desire to enter the chapel of the apparitions. . . ."

As they were leaving, following the apparition, she found herself completely healed. One hundred forty medical documents concerning her case, attesting to her illness and its cure, have been turned over to the bishop's commission studying Medjugorje.

Mrs. Diana Basile recounts the story of her healing to Bishop Pavao Zanić, Bishop of Mostar.

Bishop Frane Franić, Archbishop of Split and Makarska, declared the following to the Yugoslavian Bishops Conference on April 15, 1985:

"If several thousand persons from Split and its surroundings are persevering in prayer, Medjugorje must be thanked. I have studied the facts, I went back to the place in order to be able to tell my faithful whether or not I approved of what one takes away from a pilgrimage to Medjugorje. I assisted at the celebrations, I spoke with the visionaries, I saw the pilgrims. Medjugorje has borne the fruits of prayer, of fasting, of conversion, all fruits which are abundant and evident.

Recently Cardinal Kuharić said that one could not interdict private pilgrimages. One can freely discuss the facts regarding Medjugorje and each one is free to accept them or not. For my part, I consider that here we are dealing with supernatural events."

Bishop Franić, Archbishop of Split and Makarska and President of the Yugoslavian Bishops Commission for Doctrine and Faith, seen here with the visionaries Ivan and Marija, before an apparition.

"Fast and be converted"

"**P**ray and fast every Friday on bread and water. . . The renunciation of all sin is a true fast. Above all give up those television programs which are harmful to the family because otherwise you will lose the capacity to pray. . . ."

"No one is dispensed from fasting, except those who are gravely ill. Prayer and works of charity can not take its place."

"On Thursdays — the day consecrated to the Eucharist
— each one should find a way of giving up something:
— the one who smokes should give up smoking;
— the one who likes an alcoholic drink should give it up;
— each one should give up something that is pleasurable."

"During those forty days in the desert, Jesus had nothing to eat." (Lk 4:4)

Ivan, shown here with a friend, is faithful to his fast on bread and water.

"Reform your lives!" (Mt 3:2)

"**M**y dear children, without prayer there is no peace. For this reason I tell you to pray for peace. Pray before the crucifix."
"Even those crosses of your own making are in the plan of God. . . ."
"Climb the mountain and pray before the cross that has been set up there. You know that it represents the sacrifice of Jesus. . . . I need your prayers. . . ."
"Let everyone know as soon as possible that I desire their conversion and proclaim it alone. . . ."
"Give me your hearts! I want to change them completely. I want to remake them. I want them to be pure. You know that I love you and will protect you. . . ."
"Thank you for your sacrifices."

Every month in Medjugorje, during the three days which precede the first Sunday of the month, the parishioners carefully prepare themselves for their monthly confession.

Since the confessionals inside the church are never sufficient priests make do on chairs set up outside.

The only water fountain available to quench the thirst of the pilgrims.

A new exodus towards . . .

"**M**y dear children, reform your lives! You in the parish, take my invitation to heart. . . Thus those who come here will likewise be converted."

I know that you pray for long periods, but truly liberate yourselves.
Pray even during the evening after you have finished your day. Seat yourselves in

your room and say to Jesus: 'Thank you!' If at night you fall asleep praying, you will awake in the morning thinking of Jesus and you will be able to pray to Him for peace.

Scene of the church around which some pilgrims are seated during the celebration of the Eucharist.

But if you fall asleep with a million distractions, you will awake the next morning feeling oppressed and you may even forget to pray. . . .·Be patient, be constant!

The spirit of the world is a sinful spirit . . . It seems to you that it is not sinful because you live in an atmosphere of peace. . . . How many, though, there are who do not listen to Jesus!

If you only knew how much I suffer, you would never sin again.
I need all of your prayers.
Pray!"

Croatian women climb the hill of the apparitions barefooted and praying.

"You will be the sign . . ."

Ivanka Ivanković

"**M**y dear children! Today I invit[e]
in a special way to enter into comb[at]
with Satan by means of prayer. Sa[tan]
intends to act more forcefully agains[t]
now that you are wise to his activit[y]
Arm yourselves against him and w[ith]
the Rosary in hand you will defeat h[im]
(Aug. 8[)]

Ivanka Ivanković, who was left an orp[han]
upon the death of her mother, was bor[n]
June 6, 1966 at Bijakovići. She was the f[irst]
see the Madonna on June 24, 1981. Fo[r her]
the apparitions ceased on May 7, 1985.

Here is a description of that last apparition to Ivanka:

May 6: The Madonna appeared for about two minutes to Vicka, Jakov, Marija and Ivanka. But she continued the dialogue with Ivanka alone for another six minutes. In these eight minutes all together, the Madonna revealed the 10th secret and finished telling her about the future of the world. She then told her that on the next day she would wait for her alone at home.

May 7: Ivanka had the apparition at her own home. Regarding it, she had this to report to Father Slavko: "As usual, just as it had been on all the other days, my Mother greeted me with these words, '*May Jesus Christ be praised!*' and I answered her, 'May He always be praised!' She was with me for an hour. Never had I seen her so lovely. She was so gentle and beautiful. . . . She had the most beautiful gown which shone like silver and gold. With her were two angels and they wore the same kind of dress. I cannot find words adequate to describe all that beauty. Such moments have to be lived.

"She asked me what I most desired at the moment: I answered her, 'to see my earthly mother' [who had died a month before the apparitions of 1981]. She gave me a smile and my mother apeared. I saw her. She was radiant. The Madonna told me that I could stand up. My mother embraced me and kissed me saying: 'My daughter, I am so proud of you!' She kissed me another time and disappeared. The Madonna then contined: '*Dear child of mine, this is our last meeting. Don't be sad, because I will come back every year on the day of the anniversary of these apparitions.*

'*Don't think that you have done something bad and that this is the reason that I am not coming any more. You embraced the project which my Son and I had for you wholeheartedly. The graces which you and your companions have received, no one in this world has ever had! You must be happy. I am your Mother, and I love you with all my heart, Ivanka. I thank you because you responded to my invitation and to that of my Son and because you have been so patient and stayed with us for as long as we wished. My child, you must tell your friends that my Son and I will always be with you every time that you have need of us.*"

Ivanka asked the Madonna for permission to kiss her and her request was granted. Then Mary slowly went away. The more time passes, the more Ivanka suffers the absence of those visits with Mary. Vicka has offered to help her by praying together with her often.

Mirjana Dragičević

"**I**t's very important that you kno__
that Satan exists. He has God's
permission to test the Church, but n__
destroy it. When the secrets which __
entrusting to you come to pass, the p__
of Satan will be done away with.
For now, he has become aggressive. __
destroys marriages, sets priests aga__
one another, is responsible for many
individuals' obsessions. . . . Therefo__
protect yourself from him through pr__
and fasting; above all through
community prayer. Carry with you
keep in your homes signs of your fai__
renew your use of holy water. Satar__
cannot do anything against those u__
faith in God is strong."

(To Mir__

**Mirjana Dragičević in prayer. She is fr__
Bijakovići, but lives with her family in
Sarajevo. She received the tenth secret
December 25, 1982 and since then has
no further daily apparitions.**

Now Mary appears to her only on her birthday or on special occasions, such as happened on March 19, 1984, to clarify some details relative to the ten secrets confided to her. These have been written down on a piece of paper which, at a time that will be indicated by the Blessed Virgin, will be able to be read, by a special grace, only by Father Petar Ljubičić, chosen by Mirjana for the revelation of the secrets.

It is a piece of paper whose contents, which deal with the actual situation of the world, cause great sorrow to the Blessed Virgin Mary and bring tears to her eyes at the thought of her *"atheistic children and those who listen to her but do not reform their lives"* as well as of those *"who live only to make money."* They also cause Mirjana to weep with intense sorrow when she sees people doing what they shouldn't do.

For all of these, her children, the Virgin invites Mirjana also to pray without tiring. Thus it happened even on the occasion of the last apparition in which the Mother of God, taking the Rosary of the young girl, said to her: *"The Rosary is not an ornament. It's necessary to pray it."* The consequences are very serious. Those responsible for the Church have not yet pronounced their judgment on these matters, and, indeed, in many quarters there is a great deal of incredulity still. Many who go to Medjugorje go there out of curiosity or to ask for worldly things. The times themselves speak to us of the urgency to pray for peace and to reform our lives, but few are being converted.

On October 25, 1985 the Blessed Virgin appeared to Mirjana as she had on several occasions that year. During the seven-minute apparition, she showed her the first warning. Mirjana wept and asked, "But will this happen so quickly?" Then she added: "How can God be so hard-hearted?" The Virgin replied: *"It will all come to pass, but God is not hard-hearted. Look around you and see that men have done this and never again say that God is hard-hearted. But you mustn't be afraid because I am here."* Father Petar was present, and Mirjana will tell him about the first warning three days before it comes to pass.

"Awake, O sleeper, arise from the dead, and Christ will give you light."
(Ep 5:14)

"I came to you because I found faith here. I chose your parish and I intend to watch over it. I will care for it with love and desire that all of you be mine. I wish that those who are with me and with my Son were more numerous. . . . Tell those who do not see me that they should believe as if they did. . . ."

"As your Mother, I love each one of you at every moment. If you are in trouble, do not be afraid because I love you even then, even when you are far from me and from my Son."

"Please, I beg you! Don't let my heart weep tears of blood for the loss of souls caused by sin."

"For that reason, believe, pray and fast!"

Vicka Ivanković of Bijakovici, born September 3, 1964, is the oldest of the young visionaries, the most outgoing and the one who most willingly lends herself to answering people's questions. Her mother says of her: "The more I see my daughter suffer, the more I see her happy. I don't understand it."

Vicka Ivanković

30

Marija Pavlović, born in Bijakovići on April 1, 1965, is the one among the visionaries who, even before the apparitions, was the most faithful to prayer. Her habitual reserve often reminds people of the figure of St. Bernadette of Lourdes.

"**I** will leave a sign for nonbelievers, before which many will come to believe. Not all, however, will reform their lives. . . These, too, are my children and I suffer much for them, because they do not know what awaits them if they do not reform their lives and turn again to God. Pray! Pray! Pray!"

"Through you the people will believe. If you want to be strong in the face of evil, develop a lively conscience. I repeat: Pray in particular every morning, read a passage from the Gospel, plant the seed of God's word within you and let it come alive within you often during the day, especially during moments of discouragement and in the evening you will be stronger. . . ."

"If you want to be completely happy, live a simple and humble life. Pray a lot and don't try to delve too deeply into problems. Let God resolve them for you."

31

"**A**t the beginning, my parents would not let me climb the hill of the apparitions. Even so, I saw the Madonna at the same time that she was appearing to my friends."

Ivan Dragičević, born on May 25, 1965, also in Bijakovići, has overcome his natural timidity and given proof of a deep sense of responsibility.

Jakov Čolo

When he was ill, the Blessed Virgin gave him this message: *"Dear son! Dedicate all the prayers you recite in your home each night for the conversion of sinners because the world is immersed in serious evils. Recite the Rosary every evening."*

Jakov Čolo, the youngest of the visionaries, like Ivanka, was left orphaned by the death of his mother. He was born in Bijakovići on March 6, 1971. Notwithstanding his young age, he has reached a surprising degree of spiritual maturity.

The night between the 24th and the 25th of June, 1985, the Madonna invited the visionaries to the top of Mt. Krizevać for an extraordinary apparition.
To Ivan she said: *"I am happy above all at the large number of young people who are present."*

The rock strewn path that leads to the summit of Mt. Krizevać.

The cross erected in 1933 at the top of
Mt. Krizevać.

"Protect the faith of my people!"

Not only are the crowds of faithful enormous, but the priest concelebrants are also many.

"Dear children. You are weak because you pray so little. . . .
Satan wishes to thwart all my plans at this time. Pray that he does not succeed. . .
Take up the Gospel, believe and you will understand everything. Words are not enough. . . . you must strive to fathom their meaning in your heart.
In the name of the Lord, I have given you many messages, but you have not followed them. . . . Dear children, you do not yet know how to love nor how to listen with love to these messages. I am your Mother, and I have come to teach you all how to love, to feel and to pray with love, not because you have to but because you have problems and crosses. Every cross gives glory to the Lord. . . .

Inside the church during the distribution of Holy Communion.

Thank you for having accepted my invitation."

"**P**ray! Pray! Pray! Only in prayer will you understand my love and the love of the Lord for you.

Pray with all your heart. I am your Mother and I want to teach you something very important: how to love. Jesus was able to pray without ceasing because He had such a great thirst for God and a fathomless desire for the salvation of souls.

Prayer is a colloquy with God. . . . It enables you to understand God. . . . It makes it possible for you to enter into the fullness of joy. . . .

Prayer is life!"

"**D**ear children! I want to tell you that I
have chosen this parish and that I will
protect it with my own hands, like a little
flower struggling for its life. I invite you to
abandon yourself to me, so that I can give
you back to God pure and immaculate.
Satan has taken aim at one part of my
plans and wants to conquer all. Pray that
he not win! Thank you for taking my call
to heart."

(Aug. 1, '85)

Milka Pavlović, sister of Marija, only saw the
Madonna on June 24, 1981.

"**B**y means of assiduous prayer, I will lead you to the most profound experiences. . . . How happy I should be if all the world were to follow this path!"

Father Jozo Zovko, pastor of the parish at Medjugorje when the apparitions began, speaking here with the pastor of the parish church of Fatima (Portugal).

Two of the principal animators of the liturgy
in the parish at Medjugorje from the very
beginning of the apparitions to this day

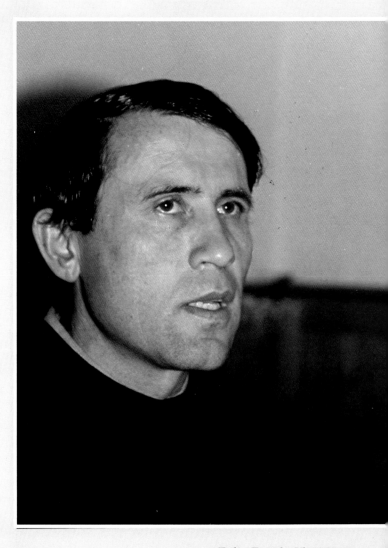

"*It is necessary to be converted to God if peace is to be had. Tell the whole world, as soon as possible, that I desire and strongly will that people reform their lives. Be converted and do not hesitate!*

I will intercede with my Son that He not punish the world. But you must reform your lives! Be detached from the things of this world and be prepared for anything that might come to pass. . . . Those who find God will find joy, and in that joy they will find true peace. Reform your lives, therefore, at once, and open your hearts to God. . . .

When the Sign appears, it will be too late for many. My children! The Holy Sacrifice of the Mass will be your gift each day. Look forward to it, desire it, because in it Jesus gives Himself to you. . . . Long ardently, therefore, for the moment of your purification. . . . Pray diligently that the Holy Spirit might renew you. . . .

If the people assist at the Mass lukewarmly, they will go home cold and with an empty heart. I so wish that your hearts might be united to mine, as my heart is united to that of my Son."

Father Tomislav Vlasić. He was sent to
Medjugorje when the pastor, Father Jozo, was
put in jail.
"At the first announcement regarding the
apparitions, I said: 'The Gospel is enough for
me. I believe. I have no need of apparitions.'
Then I saw how pharisaical that was; even now
I realize how very far I am from God,
because the road opens before me ever more
and more. . . .'

"**F**or all, the most important thing is to enter profoundly into prayer. . . . Afterwards, one's choices will be correctly made.

Don't worry about the future. . . . I will lead all of you. Begin by invoking the Holy Spirit each day. The essential thing is to pray to Him. . . . then everything will become clear, everything will be transformed.

Prayer always leaves one in peace and serenity. My wish is that everyone might keep an image of the Sacred Heart in their homes and recite the Rosary in its entirety.

Those who abandon themselves entirely into the hands of God no longer have any room in their hearts for fear. . . . The difficulties that you may have will be a source of growth for you and an occasion for giving glory to God. . . .

So have no fear! You must offer in your prayers all your work and all your plans. Each day offer everything to Jesus and give it all to Him in your prayer, thanking Him. . . .

Accept life as Jesus tells you to: with abandonment into His hands. Then the people will understand what you are living for and will be converted by your testimony. If you want to understand my love, then pray!"

Father Slavko Barbarić.

Having succeeded Father Tomislav as the one in charge of the pilgrims who come to Medjugorje, he has made a rigorously scientific study of the psychology of the group which has formed itself around Mary. He says: Medjugorje does not depend on the visionaries nor on the priests who work here."

Pilgrims listening to information regarding the events which are said to have been transpiring at Medjugorje.

"**T**he messages which I have transmitted on the part of my Son are for everybody, but in a special way for the Holy Father, and through him for all the world. . . .
From Medjugorje I want to say to the Holy Father: The word which I have come to announce is PEACE! It is my desire that he transmit this message to all the world . . . that he be courageous in announcing peace and love to all the world. . . .
May he not feel himself to be the father of Catholics only, but of all peoples. . . .
My message to him is that he strive to reunite all Christians with his preaching and that he transmit to young people that which God inspires him to say in his prayers."

"The Spirit of God will suggest what you must say!"
(Jn 14:26)

"**P**ray that the Holy Spirit might illuminate you so that you can understand. . . .
You ask for many things. . . . Ask rather for the Holy Spirit: if He comes, all the rest will be given you besides.
Our job is to accept God's peace, to live it, and to spread it, not with words, but with our lives.
Christians are wrong when, looking to the future they think of war and of evil.
For a Christian there is only one stance to take with regard to the future: it is that of hope in salvation. . . ."

From every part of the world people flock to Medjugorje. Here we see a Chinese priest in prayer.

Four successive moments during the apparitions.

1. The prayers at the beginning of each apparition.

. During the ecstasy.

3. The word "ODITE" ("You may go now") follows the termination of the apparition.

The children at the end of the
apparition still concentrating on what
inspired in their vision of the
Madonna.

47

"You are a chosen people . . ."

"**I** have chosen you and I want to lead all of you in this parish with love, and to take care of you so that all of you might be mine!
I thank you for your response to my call. I will give you a message every Thursday. . . .
Many of you, following the others, have begun to pray . . . but pray with your heart. Don't let prayer and fasting become just a habit.
Thank the Lord because he has allowed me to remain so long with you. Pray! Pray! Pray! What I do depends to a great extent on you. . . . If you knew the gift which God is offering you . . . you would pray for the rest of your life. . . . Never tire of adoring the Blessed Sacrament. . . . I am always present at such times . . . and in these moments special graces are received."

The church at Medjugorje seen from the rear.

"Dear children! I ask you not to complain, but to pray for the unity of this parish because my Son and I have special plans for this community. . . . Today I am very pleased with you and thank you for your prayers.
Pray more for the conversion of sinners. . . . With love you will obtain all things, even that which some hold to be impossible. . . . God wishes this church to belong entirely to Him, and for this reason He has sent me to you. . . .
I love you and in a special way I invite you to be the light borne to those who are in darkness. God grants each person the possibility of knowing good from evil and the strength to choose between them. . . .
Accept me then, my children! I stand before many hearts but few there are who open to me. . . . Pray that the world might accept my love!"

The statue of the Immaculate Conception placed once again in the center of the church in April of 1985.

49

The beginning of a new era for the Church

The church on the occasion of the anniversary of the apparitions no longer holds the pilgrims who pour out of the church and beyond the parish house.

Medjugorje, blossom of the Church's renewed youth.   51

"**I** want you, my dear children, to listen to my messages and to live them!
Every family ought to pray and to read the Bible together. . . . I invite you to renew yourselves in prayer.
The devil makes himself strong and with his astuteness hopes to impede my plans by seeking to discourage you. . . . He has a great deal of influence in the world. . . Thus you must pray all the more. . . . Pray with love. . . Be prudent. . . . I have stayed a long time with you in order to help you through this test. . . . Pray to the Holy Spirit that you might succeed in transmitting my messages as they are given to you. . . . I, your Mother, tell you that you pray very little. . . . I want to repeat that you should open your hearts to God as the flowers of Spring open to the sun. . . . I want you to be always close to your heavenly Father, that He might fill you with His graces. I thank you for taking my call to heart!"

The apparitions on April 4, 1985 took place in the parish house.

"**M**y babies! I invite you to live the following words: I love God! Love of God is not widespread in the world. So pray! I have nothing else to tell you: Pray! Pray! Pray! Go into your homes and pray before the crucifix. I am with you even in the smallest trials. . . . I need your prayers. . . . Help me!"

(Christmas 1984) *"Dear children! I invite you to take a concrete step for Jesus. I want each family in the parish to place a flower next to the crib for Jesus as a sign of its abandonment to Him. I want each member of the family to deposit his or her own flower next to the crib for Jesus who is to come. . . . Like any loving Mother, we must prepare ourselves for this Son who is coming. . . ."*

"For a child is born to us. . . . They name him . . . Prince of Peace!"   (Is 9:5)

"The day of my two-thousandth birthday falls on the fifth of August 1984. Three days before, do not work. Just pray. Take the Rosary in your hands and . . . Pray! Pray! Pray!

I have dedicated my whole life to you. Now you must dedicate at least three days to me.

. . . That day is a very special gift of my Son Jesus to console me.

There will be great conversions throughout the world. . . . I know that all the families of the parish can spend four hours a day, which is just one-sixth of the day, in prayer. . . .

Dear children! At this time Satan wants to thwart all my plans. . . . Pray so that he does not succeed. Help me with your prayers so that I may win. . . ."

(to Jelena)

One day Jelena asked the Madonna, "Why are you so beautiful?"

"Because I love. If you want to become beautiful like me, you must love.

But love is a grace of the Lord. It is a gift of the Spirit. You cannot buy it nor can you give it to someone else. All those who open themselves to God can have it."

Jelena Vasilj during a moment of deep contemplation.

August 15, 1985: *"Dear children! I bless you and wish to tell you that I love you. And I invite you to live my messages. Today I bless all of you with the solemn benediction which the Omnipotent has conceded to me. Thank you for having responded to my call."*

Marijana's amiability is apparent in her expression.

"... then will you live a life of love and abandonment"

The visionaries recite the seven 'Our Father's, 'Hail Mary's and 'Glory Be's wit[h] Father Jozo Zovko and the people.

"**T**urn over your hearts like you turn over the soil of your fields... Don't desire to move about in these days in which the Holy Spirit is working in such a powerful way.... Your hearts are taken up with the things of earth and these preoccupy you....

Turn your hearts to prayer and seek for the Holy Spirit to pour Himself out upon you! Persons who decide to belong totally

The curious who climb over one another to peer
through a small window in the chapel during
one of the apparitions.

"Love drives away all fear"

"**I** recommend group participation at prayer, especially to the young who are freer and can give themselves to prayer at least three hours a day.

1. Renounce all disordered passions.
2. Abandon yourselves totally to God.
3. Get rid of all fear once and for all. I will lead your group for four years and will purify it. . . .

The sole means for purifying one's heart is prayer . . . right up until you reach the moment in which you are totally present to God. . . .

When you sin, it is as if you had fainted or lost consciousness . . . and your fears keep you far from me and you think of me as a very severe person, or as someone very distant to you. . . .

Pray! And I will pray with you!"

Vicka during an apparition at her own home.

The ever smiling face of Vicka.

"You don't realize how great the mercy of God is towards you! . . . Thank Him for having allowed me to remain for such a long while with you!
. . . Now I invite you to love; love in the first place your own families and then you will be able to accept with love all those who will come here. . . Dear children, open your hearts to the Lord of all hearts. Reveal to me all your sentiments and all your problems. I want to console you in your temptations. I want to fill you with peace, with joy, and with the love of God. If you knew how much I loved you, you would weep for joy."

"**I** *want this church to become a source of grace for all.*"

Medjugorje at sunset.

Where Mary speaks, her children gather.

Objects placed on the altar during the
apparition to be blessed.

"**D**ear children, today I invite you to
make wide use in your homes of sacred
objects. Carry on your persons blessed
sacred signs, so that, thus armed against
him, Satan may tempt you less."

Doctor Frigerio (first on the right) and a team of doctors examine Marija and Jakov.

Some doctors at Medjugorje. A French team under the direction of Doctor Joyeux and an Italian team under the direction of Doctor Frigerio have carefully examined the visionaries during the apparitions with the aid of sophisticated apparatus. Their conclusions exclude all forms of fakery or hallucination.

"**D**ear little ones, today I wish to tell you that God wants to test you; you will come through it well if you pray. God tests you through the things which happen to you each day. So pray now that you may pass this test. From all that God gives you by means of these tests, you will be able to come out of them more open to Him. Seek to grow closer to God with love. I thank you for having accepted my invitation."

(Aug. 22, '85)

The six visionaries, whom the Virgin calls, "My Angels!" sing and pray during a religious function in the first year of the apparitions.

Characteristics of the Messages

In all apparitions there are certain special characteristics. Naturally these do nothing more than emphasize one aspect or another of Revelation inasmuch as Christ is "the Mediator and at the same time the fullness of all Revelation," and "we now await no new further public revelation before the glorious manifestation of our Lord Jesus Christ" (*Dei Verbum*, 2 and 4).

The messages of the Blessed Virgin are very brief if they are taken one by one. They are more numerous than usual and it is at once apparent that all of the points emphasized are to be found in Revelation. Here, though, they take on an accent not found in other apparitions. Their principal characteristics are:

1. The appeal for peace is constantly repeated. The woman of the vision even calls herself *"The Queen of Peace."* All the messages seem to be centered around this theme of peace: a return to God, a sincere conversion, prayer, fasting, etc. The theme of peace constitutes in the eyes of most what is the essential in these apparitions.

2. *"God exists. In him everything has life. The one who finds God finds life."* The existence of God is the fundamental presupposition of religion; other apparitions have never insisted on this point. But it has become urgent for our day and age, marked as it is by mass taught atheism. This is one of the main characteristics of Medjugorje, like the insistence on the praying of the Creed, a synthesis of the truths of our faith.

3. *Prayer, fasting, sacraments.* These have been the constant appeals of the latest apparitions approved by the Church: La Salette, Lourdes, Fatima. Here, though, there is something new: examples are furnished and precise details given.

Regarding prayer: as a minimum the daily recitation of seven 'Our Father's, 'Hail Mary's, 'Glory Be's and one 'Creed' is advised; but a half-hour of prayer morning and evening is also recommended. A more prolonged prayer is advised for those who are able. The Rosary is important: *"Call people back to praying the Rosary." "I say to all priests, 'Pray the Rosary. Dedicate time to its recitation.'"*

Fasting: a bread and water fast is suggested, for those who are more generous, and not only on Fridays.

Mass and the Sacraments: assistance at daily Mass is encouraged. Regarding the Sacrament of Reconciliation: *"If Christians go to their confessor once a month, soon whole regions will be healed spiritually."*

4. Other evangelical truths are also recalled with insistence: *the last ends, the judgment of God, the existence of Satan*. The precepts of the Lord keep coming up, especially on charity, notably in its most difficult and heroic form, *love for one's enemies*. In all of this one cannot help but see an invitation to universal brotherhood. The Virgin presents herself as the *Mother of all*, just as God is the *Father of all*. Nor can one help but see in this teaching a confirmation of the ecumenical spirit of the Second Vatican Council, especially if one considers that this invitation is made in Yugoslavia where Catholics, Orthodox, Muslims and atheists live side by side. All these teachings obviously conform to the Gospels and to the practice of the Church. No new devotion is suggested here, nor is any new practice introduced.

The Signs and the Secrets

From the very first days of the apparitions the visionaries asked the Blessed Virgin to show herself to all those persons present or to give a sign so that others might believe in her, because they were treating them like liars and accusing them of having invented everything. And so Our Lady has promised that she will cause a *sign* to suddenly appear on Podbrdo hill. She has revealed the date to the visionaries and shown it to them. They say that it is something tangible, stable and indestructible.

She also promised to tell each one of them ten secrets. As far as we know, they are not the same for all. Certain secrets have a personal character. For the most part they concern the future. Mirjana indicates that there will be two warnings, then the *sign* will appear. If people do not reform their lives, the chastisement will follow. She recommends that all reform their lives at once: *"When the sign appears, it will be too late for many."*

Why, one wonders, at Medjugorje as at La Salette and at Fatima, are secrets concerning the future announced without being divulged? In the light of the Bible it seems that we might be able to respond in this way: the matters treated are not inevitable (one thinks of the preaching of Jonah about the destruction of Nineveh), but they are things which conversion and prayer can change or at least attenuate. It seems also that they serve another objective: when dealing with a state of eschatological tension, they direct our gaze towards the final coming of Christ the Lord, just as was the case at the time of the first Christians.

The Confidants of Mary

The boys and girls chosen by Our Lady have taken part in an exceptional spiritual itinerary. We see them here at the time of the beginning of the apparitions. The smallest, Jakov, was only ten; Vicka was seventeen.

In these years they have changed a lot. Their prayer has become one of stupefying intensity. But one is struck most by the great charity with which they receive pilgrims, by whom they are veritably sieged to the point of no longer having the least liberty to take care of their own personal business. And that is not all. What most amazes one about these youngsters is their spirit of sacrifice and reparation. The case of Vicka is typical. She has offered herself for the conversion of sinners. She had excellent health. Now she suffers headaches which torment her night and day. But this suffering has not robbed her of her characteristic smile.

The group of six visionaries who got together on June 25, 1981, on the second day of their meetings with the Blessed Virgin. They include (from left to right): Mirjana, Vicka, Ivanka, Ivan, Marija, and in front of them all, little Jakov.

Conclusion

According to the information furnished by the Yugoslavian authorities and rendered public in a television transmission in October of 1986, more than seven million pilgrims have already paid a visit to Medjugorje. Many of them have but one desire, and that is to return. By means of the pages of this album we, too, have seen the places and taken note of the messages. We know that many Christians who have not been able to go to the place have still understood the importance of the messages and have formed prayer groups. There have been moving conversions of many persons who have never made the trip to Medjugorje and who have only heard about the apparitions of "The Queen of Peace." This is Mary's hour. It is the time for men to turn back to God.

Some would prefer to wait for the ecclesiastical authorities to speak out. But that is going to take time. Meanwhile, the content of the message is evangelical, and the Gospel must be put into practice without delay. It cannot wait. The parables of Jesus multiply warnings for those who beat about the bush or elude the appeals of God. Remember those invited to the wedding feast who presented pretext after pretext in order to decline the invitation; the foolish maidens in waiting who arrived after the door had been closed; the servant who buried his talent?

When Jesus came to earth, the angels sang: "Glory to God in the highest, and peace on earth to men of good will." The message of Medjugorje can be summed up as an appeal to render glory to God so that peace might indeed reign on earth. If one looks at the world closely, one cannot help but see that peace on earth is in dire peril. One can no longer ignore the fact that our scientific progress has forged an age of terrifying destruction; the disasters which would befall mankind in the case of nuclear war are unimaginable.

The Blessed Virgin has not come to predict catastrophes, but to teach us how to avoid them. At Fatima she predicted: "In the end, my Immaculate Heart will triumph." At Medjugorje she has shown this — it seems — with a frequency which has no precedence in the history of the Church. The main message lies in her very presence, and only then in the invitation to follow her recommendations. At Lourdes, the Virgin appeared at the break of dawn; at Fatima, she appeared at noon. In Medjugorje, she appears as the sun begins to set. History's clock stresses time's inevitability. "Happy the servant whom the Master finds watching when he returns." The Mother of the Church is getting us ready to welcome Jesus her Son.

Epilogue to the English Language Edition

If the authenticity of reported apparitions were to be judged by their spiritual fruits, there seems little doubt that the events which have been transpiring in Medjugorje have about them the ring of authenticity. The parish of Medjugorje has been transformed. Each evening there is a reconciliation service at the church with up to as many as thirty priests hearing confessions at one time. Most, if not all the families, have accepted Mary's call to fast on Fridays and to be faithful to the family recitation of the Rosary. Masses are crowded. Conversions are common. An atmosphere of forgiveness and peace reigns everywhere.

We know, however, that the Church very prudently reserves judgment in cases such as these because of the very real danger of mass hysteria and delusion. A commission has been appointed by the local bishop to investigate the matter, and as of this date, their report has not yet appeared.

While waiting official recognition of the apparitions from the Church, the editor of the present volume has tried to present a moving description in word and picture of what many feel to be one of the most extraordinary religious occurrences of the decade. May this book contribute in some small way to the peace and salvation of the world.

Solemnity of the Mother of God
January 1, 1987